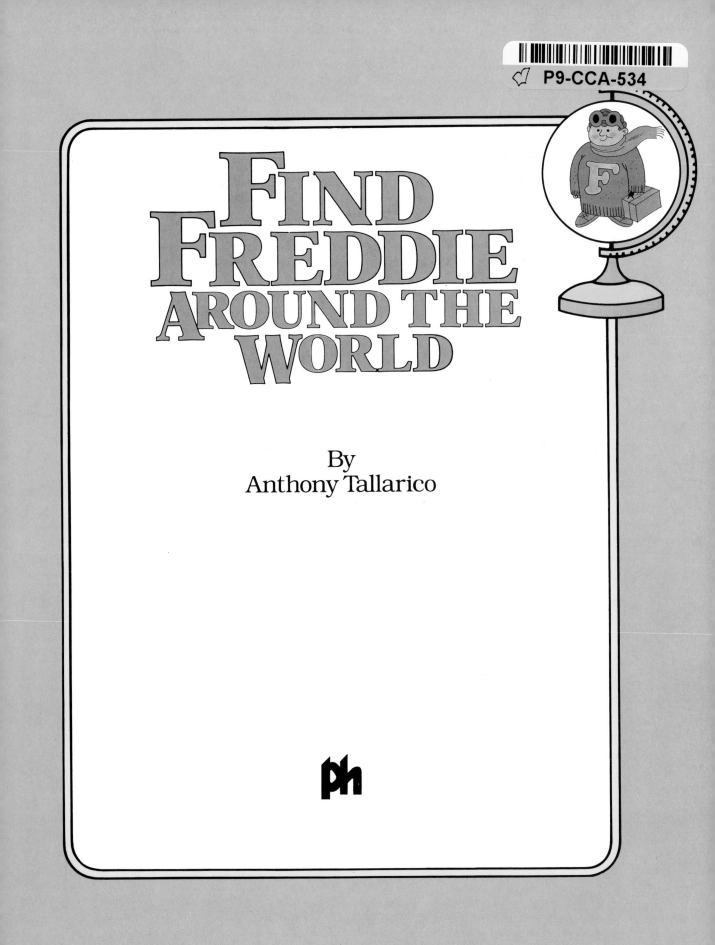

FIND FREDDIE AROUND THE WORLD

By
Anthony Tallarico

ph

Freddie has won an around the world vacation…and you're invited to come along! Stay close to Freddie, or you might get lost!

FIND FREDDIE IN THE UNITED STATES AND…

- ☑ Balloons (2)
- ☑ Barn
- ☑ Brooms (2)
- ☑ Buffalo
- ☑ Cactus (4)
- ☑ Campfire
- ☑ Cannon
- ☑ Cows (2)
- ☑ Coyote
- ☑ Footballs (2)
- ☑ Ghost
- ☑ Goat
- ☑ Guitars (2)
- ☑ Hockey player
- ☑ Jack-o´-lantern
- ☑ Kite
- ☑ Lighthouse
- ☑ Log cabin
- ☑ Moose
- ☑ Owl
- ☑ Periscope
- ☑ Scarecrows (2)
- ☑ Star
- ☑ Statue of Liberty
- ☑ Surfer
- ☑ Turtle
- ☑ Witch

Where did the ~~San Diego Zoo~~
    elephant escape from?
Who is sleeping?
Where is Cuba? ~~Coran Island~~
What's on sale?
Where's the big cheese?

Freddie is northward bound as he travels to Canada, Alaska, Greenland and Iceland.

FIND FREDDIE IN THIS WINTER WONDERLAND AND...

- ☐ Banana skin
- ☐ Bear
- ☐ Beaver
- ☐ Birds (2)
- ☐ Bone
- ☐ Box
- ☐ Bucket
- ☐ Car
- ☐ Elephant
- ☐ Elf
- ☐ Hare
- ☐ Horse
- ☐ Ice-cream cone
- ☐ Igloo
- ☐ Jester
- ☐ King Kong
- ☐ Lumberjack
- ☐ Mountie
- ☐ Oil well
- ☐ Pencil
- ☐ Pumpkin
- ☐ Scarecrow
- ☐ Seal
- ☐ Sledges (2)
- ☐ Snow castle
- ☐ Snowmen (2)
- ☐ Stars (2)
- ☐ Top hat
- ☐ Totem pole
- ☐ Unicycle

What's on sale?
Where did Freddie take
  French lessons?
What's the 49th state?
Where's Greenland?
What's the capital of
  Canada?
Where's Nova Scotia?

Freddie heads south-east to the next four stops on his world tour: England, Scotland, Ireland and Wales.

FIND FREDDIE IN THE BRITISH ISLES AND...

- Aeroplane
- Bagpiper
- Boats (7)
- Book
- Broom
- Bus
- Chicken
- Crown
- Dog
- Fish (8)
- Four-leaf clovers (4)
- Guitar
- Harp
- Horseshoe
- Kite
- Knight
- Magnifying glass
- Periscope
- Pig
- Pot of gold
- Sheep (3)
- Spear
- Stonehenge
- Telescope
- Turtle
- Umbrella

What games are they playing? (4)
What's for sale (2)?
Where's France?
Who did Freddie visit in Ireland?

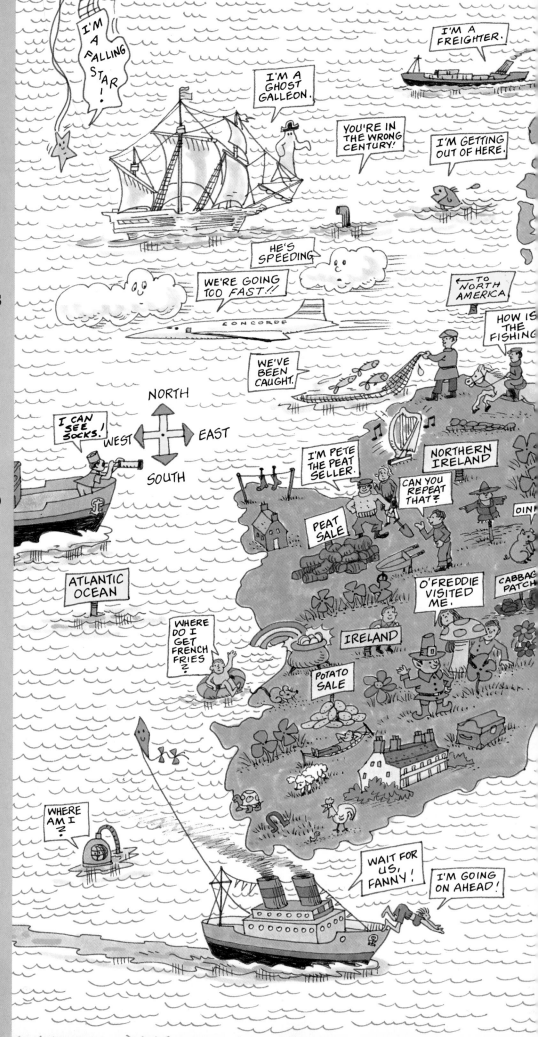

Freddie travels on throughout Europe... and you go along with him!

FIND FREDDIE AMONG THESE FRIENDLY FOREIGNERS AND...

- ☑ Artist
- ☐ Bather
- ☐ Beach ball
- ☐ Bone
- ☑ Bull
- ☐ Camel
- ☑ Castle
- ☑ Dogs (2)
- ☑ Envelope
- ☑ Fire hydrant
- ☑ Hare
- ☑ Heart
- ☑ Jack-o'-lantern
- ☑ Key
- ☑ Laundry
- ☑ Motorcycle
- ☑ Mountain goat
- ☑ Pencil
- ☑ Sailboats (2)
- ☑ Santa Claus
- ☑ Skier
- ☑ Snowmen (2)
- ☐ Stars (2)
- ☑ Stork
- ☑ Tulip
- ☑ Turtles (2)
- ☑ Volcano
- ☑ Witch

Who was forgotten?
What gets wet?
Where do pandas live?
Where's the Strait of Gibraltar?

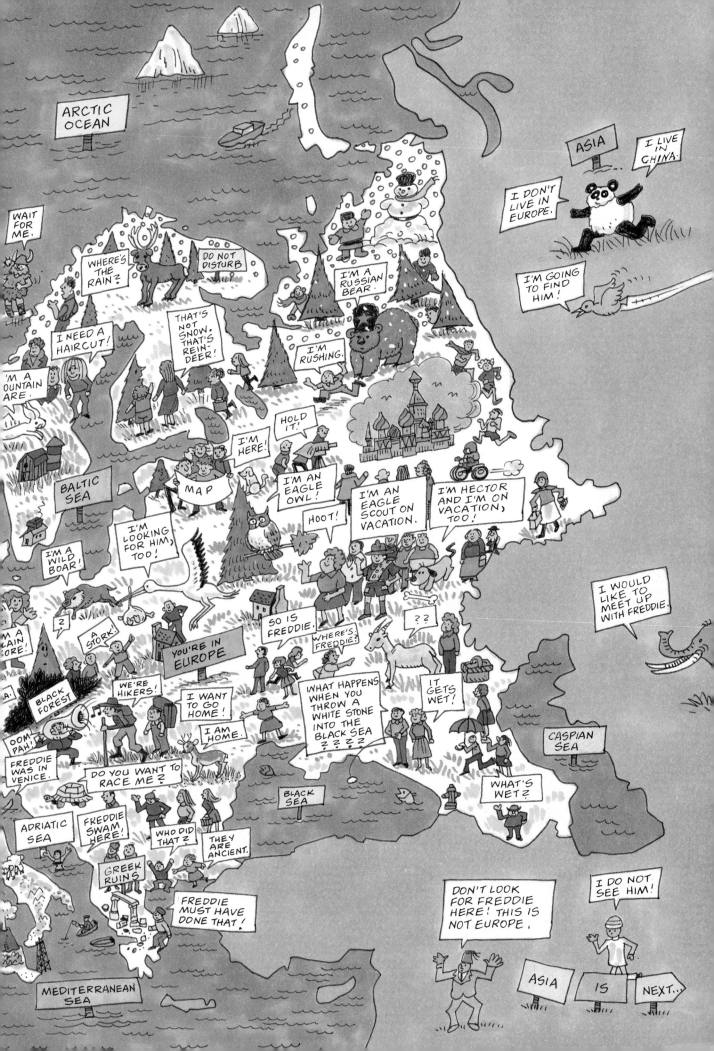

Next, Freddie is off to explore the largest continent, Asia. There are many things here that he's always wanted to see..

FIND FREDDIE IN THIS VAST AND EXOTIC LAND AND...

- ☐ Accordion
- ☐ Balloon
- ☐ Bears (2)
- ☐ Bird cage
- ☐ Candy cane
- ☐ Chef
- ☐ Dragon
- ☐ Fan
- ☐ Flying carpet
- ☐ Genie
- ☐ Heart
- ☐ Horse
- ☐ Kite
- ☐ Lemming
- ☐ Nutmeg tree
- ☐ Pandas (3)
- ☐ Peacock
- ☐ Reindeer
- ☐ Rice field
- ☐ Snakes (2)
- ☐ Surfer
- ☐ Tea cup
- ☐ Tears
- ☐ Telescope
- ☐ Tigers (2)
- ☐ Turtle
- ☐ Tyre
- ☐ Water buffalo
- ☐ Yak

Where is the highest place on earth?
Which way is the North Pole?
Where's Japan?
Who needs the oasis?

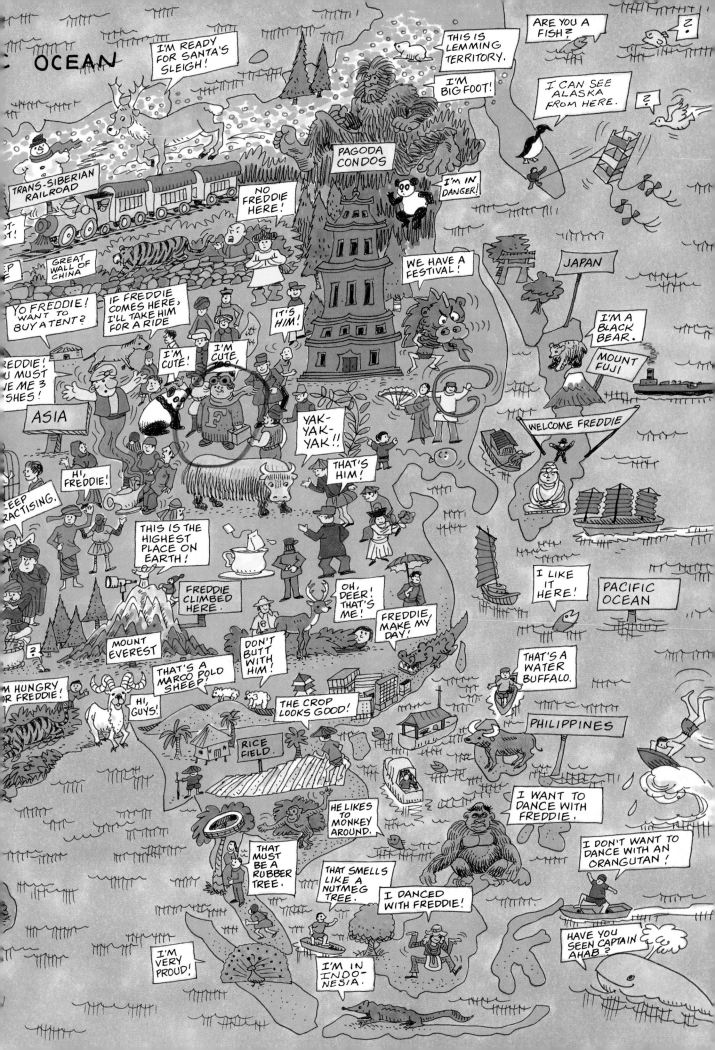

Freddie's next stop is a continent filled with amazing animals. I hope he doesn't get into any trouble there.

FIND FREDDIE IN THIS AFRICAN ADVENTURE-LAND AND...

- ☑ Aardvark
- ☑ Book
- ☑ Boot
- ☐ Bottle
- ☑ Camels (2)
- ☑ Cape buffalo
- ☑ Cape seal
- ☑ Car
- ☑ Crocodile
- ☐ Cup
- ☑ Date palm
- ☐ Drum
- ☑ Giraffes (2)
- ☐ Gnu
- ☑ Gorilla
- ☑ Heart
- ☑ Huts (4)
- ☐ Ibis
- ☑ Leopard
- ☑ Light bulb
- ☑ Monkeys (3)
- ☑ Ostrich
- ☑ Pelican
- ☑ Penguin
- ☑ Porcupine
- ☑ Rhino
- ☑ Snakes (3)
- ☑ Sunglasses (4)
- ☑ Top hat
- ☑ TV antennas
- ☑ Umbrella

Who's the king of the jungle?
Who's wearing stripes?
Where's the Suez Canal?

Freddie arrives in Australia and takes a very interesting ride. He'll stop off in New Zealand, New Guinea, and Tasmania, too.

FIND FREDDIE IN THE LAND DOWN UNDER AND...

☐ Baseball bat
☐ Book
☐ Boomerang
☐ Chef
☐ Crane
☐ Dingo
☐ Dragon
☐ Dumb-bells
☐ Fishermen (2)
☐ Football
☐ Ghost
☐ Golfer
☐ Horse
☐ Jogger
☐ Kite
☐ Koalas (3)
☐ Lost shorts
☐ Lost sock
☐ Lyrebird
☐ Paper aeroplane
☐ Rabbits (4)
☐ Scuba diver
☐ Shark fins (5)
☐ Sheep (4)
☐ Skateboard
☐ Stars (3)
☐ Tennis players (4)
☐ Tent
☐ Tree kangaroo
☐ Tyre
☐ Umbrella
☐ Wombat

Which three birds can't fly?
What's on sale?
Where's the Great Barrier Reef?

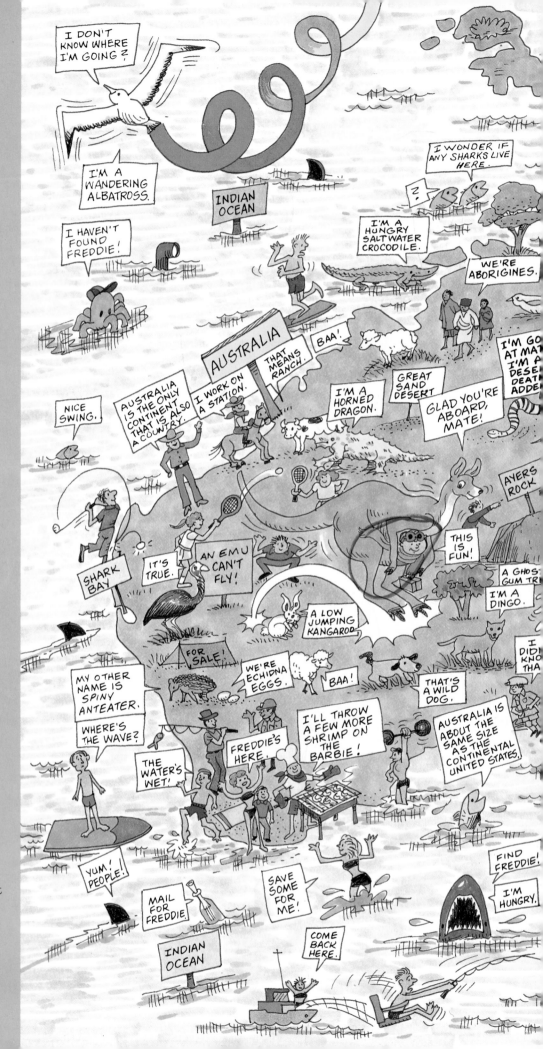

Freddie's next stop is the continent that surrounds the South Pole – Antarctica! It's the coldest place in the world. Is Freddie dressed for it?

FIND FREDDIE IN THIS BLISTERY BLIZZARD AND...

- ☑ Artist
- ☑ Balloon
- ☑ Beachball
- ☑ Bottle
- ☑ Camel
- ☐ Chair
- ☐ Chef
- ☑ Earmuffs
- ☑ Fish (2)
- ☐ Icebergs (4)
- ☑ Jester
- ☑ Key
- ☑ Lost boot
- ☑ Lost mitten
- ☑ Magnifying glass
- ☑ Palm tree
- ☑ Penguins (10)
- ☐ Pick
- ☑ Post box
- ☐ Refrigerator
- ☐ Seals (4)
- ☐ Shovel
- ☐ Skaters (3)
- ☐ Snowmen (2)
- ☑ South Pole
- ☐ Surfboard
- ☐ Telescope
- ☐ Tents (4)
- ☐ Tyre
- ☐ Whales (4)

What two things are for sale? Coke
Who's from another planet?

Watch out fourth largest continent, Freddie is coming to visit!

FIND FREDDIE IN SOUTH AMERICA AND...

☐ Alpaca
☐ Anteater
☐ Bear
☐ Binoculars
☐ Bone
☐ Bus
☐ Cactus
☐ Coffee pot
☐ Cowboy
☐ Flamingos (2)
☐ Flying bats (2)
☐ Guitar
☐ Hammock
☐ Jeep
☐ Monkeys (3)
☐ Motorcycle
☐ Oilskins
☐ Orchid
☐ Periscope
☐ Pineapple
☐ Santa Claus
☐ Snakes (4)
☐ Swamp deer
☐ Toucans (2)
☐ Tree frog
☐ Turtles (2)
☐ TV antenna
☐ Tyres (2)
☐ Umbrellas (2)
☐ Wagon

What is the longest mountain range in the world?
What's a three-sided nut?

Freddie has finally come home. All his "Where Are They?" friends are happy to see him!

FIND FREDDIE AND...

- ☐ Baseball cap
- ☑ Book
- ☑ Candy cane
- ☑ Cheese
- ☑ Dish
- ☑ Feather
- ☑ Fork
- ☑ Four-leaf clover
- ☑ Hearts (2)
- ☐ Letter
- ☑ Lost sock
- ☑ Pig
- ☑ Rug
- ☐ Slipper
- ☐ Star

What's for sale? _a condo_
Who missed Freddie the most? _Hector_

FIND FREDDIE AROUND THE WORLD

Rabén & Sjögren Bokförlag, Stockholm
www.raben.se

Originally published in Sweden by Rabén & Sjögren under the title *Mirabell*
Text copyright © 1949 by Astrid Lindgren/© 1998 Saltkråkan AB, SE-181 10 Lidingö
Pictures copyright © 2002 by Pija Lindenbaum
Library of Congress Control Number: 2002109123
Printed in Italy
First American edition, 2003
ISBN 91-29-65821-7

ASTRID LINDGREN

Pictures by Pija Lindenbaum

Mirabelle

Translated by Elisabeth Kallick Dyssegaard

R&S
BOOKS

Stockholm   New York   London   Adelaide   Toronto

I'M GOING TO TELL YOU about the strangest thing that has ever happened to me. It was two years ago, when I was just six. Now I'm eight.

My name is Britta, although that really isn't part of the story. Mama and Papa and I live in a tiny house with a little garden around it. Our house is far away from everything, and no one lives nearby. But a narrow lane passes by our house, and at the end of that lane—far away—is a town. Papa is a gardener. And every Wednesday and Saturday he drives into that town to sell vegetables and flowers at the market.

He gets paid for the things he grows, but he doesn't get
a whole lot of money. Mama says it's impossible to make
the money last. At that time—two years ago—I longed so
terribly much for a doll. I usually went with Mama and
Papa to town on market days. There is a big toy store
near the market. And every time I went by the toy store,
I looked at all the dolls and wished I could buy one.

But Mama said it was out of the question, because we
had to use all the money Papa got for the vegetables to
buy food and clothing and other things we needed. I
knew it was hopeless to think of getting a doll, but I
couldn't help wishing.

Now I'm coming to the weird part. One day in the spring Papa and Mama had gone to the market as usual with cowslips and flowering birch branches. I don't know why, but I stayed home. How lucky it was that I did! Toward evening, when it was starting to get dark, I went out front to the garden to wait for Papa and Mama.

It was a strange evening. The garden and our house and the lane—everything looked so different. There was something unusual in the air. I can't explain how peculiar it was. Just as I was looking down the lane, I heard the sound of a horse's hooves, and I was happy because I thought that Mama and Papa were coming.

But it wasn't them. It was an odd little old man who came driving around the bend. I was still standing inside the garden and watched as the cart got closer and closer. But then I came to my senses and ran to open the gate across the lane for the old man so he wouldn't have to get down. I usually opened it when someone drove by, because it was very close to our house. Sometimes I would even get a little money for doing so. When I unlatched it for the odd little old man, I was a tiny bit scared because I was all alone and I didn't know whether he was a nice old man or not. But he looked nice. And when he had driven through the gate, he halted his horse.

He looked at me and laughed, and said, "You should really get some gate money. But I don't have any, so I'll give you something else instead. Hold out your hand!"

I did. And then the old man placed a little yellow seed in my hand. It shone like gold.

"Plant this seed in your garden, and if you water it properly every day, you'll see something funny," said the old man.

Then he cracked his whip, and after a little while the cart disappeared. But I stood for a long time and heard the wheels roll and the horse trotting far away. Everything was so strange.

Finally I went to my garden
behind the house, and I
planted the yellow seed.
I fetched my green
watering can and
thoroughly watered
the place where I had
planted it.

Every day for a long time
after that, I walked around,
waiting, and I was very curious to
see what would sprout. I thought it might be a rosebush or some
other pretty plant. But I never, ever would have guessed
what it would be.

ONE MORNING, WHEN I went out to water as usual, I saw that a tiny bit of something red was sticking up out of the ground. Every day the red thing became larger and larger, until at last you could see what it was. Do you want to guess? It was a red doll's hat. And the doll's hat was attached to a doll. Yes, it was a doll growing in my garden.

Isn't that strange? Do you think I watered it?

I watered it morning, noon, and night, so that Mama and Papa said, "Sweetie, what a lot of watering! Radishes don't need that much water!"

But they never went to look, because my garden is a bit out of the way.

One morning you could see the doll's entire head. She was a blinking doll, and her eyes were shut.

She was the most beautiful doll I had ever seen. She had blond curly hair under the red hat, pink cheeks, and a red mouth.

Slowly the entire body grew. She
had a really pretty red dress
made of the same fabric
as the hat. When the doll had
grown to her knees, I told
Mama and Papa that they
should come see what was
growing in my garden. They
probably thought that it
was radishes and spinach,
but they came anyway.
I have never seen anyone as
amazed as Mama and Papa when
they saw the doll. They stood for a
long time staring.

Then Papa said, "I have never seen anything
like this!"

And Mama said, "How did this happen?"

"I planted a doll seed," I said.

And Papa said he wished he had a whole pound of
doll seeds because then he could sell a lot of dolls at
the market, and he would earn a lot more money than
he did from the radishes. For a whole day Mama and
Papa walked around amazed.

Aɴᴅ ɢᴜᴇss ᴡʜᴀᴛ! Oɴᴇ Sᴜɴᴅᴀʏ ᴍᴏʀɴɪɴɢ when I came out to my garden, the doll had finished growing. She had nice white socks and small white shoes on her feet. I sat down in the grass to get a good look at how lovely she was. And then—at that very moment—she opened her eyes and looked straight at me. She had blue eyes, exactly as I had expected. I had never seen such a wonderful doll, and I couldn't help touching her gently. But then she broke off at the root. I understood that I was meant to take her.

And I did. I ran right away to show her to Mama and Papa. And later I took her into my room and put her to bed in the cover of Mama's sewing machine, because I had no doll's bed for her. All day I played with her, and I was so happy that I could barely eat. I called her Margaret.

When evening came, I tucked her into the sewing machine cover and whispered, "Good night, Margaret!"

But do you know what happened then? She opened her mouth and said, "My name is not Margaret. My name is Mirabelle."

Just think, she could talk! She was a real chatterbox, and I was so surprised that I almost couldn't answer. She said that she wanted a proper bed and a nightgown. And she added that she liked me very much and would like to have me as a mama.

"But don't ever try to feed me oatmeal," she said. "Because I don't eat it."

I needed to think, so I crept into my own bed and lay there completely silent.

Mirabelle was also silent. But soon I saw why. She was trying to climb up the dresser. And she did. When she got up on top of the dresser, she jumped down into her bed—I mean the sewing machine cover. She did it several times, then laughed delightedly and said, "That was fun!"

After a little while she came over to my bed and asked, "Can I sleep in your bed with you? You are my mama now."

I lifted her up into my bed, and she lay there and talked. It was so nice to listen to her.

I was so happy about Mirabelle; I had never been so happy in my whole life. At last she stopped talking. She yawned a few times—it looked so sweet!—then she cuddled up against my arm and fell asleep. I didn't have the heart to move her. She lay there all night. I stayed awake for a long time and listened to her breathing in the dark.

When I woke up in the morning, Mirabelle had climbed up onto the little table next to my bed. There was a glass of water on it. Mirabelle poured out all of the water. Then she laughed and jumped into the sewing machine cover. Mama came in right after, and Mirabelle lay there and looked just like an ordinary doll.

Now I have had Mirabelle for two years. And I don't think there is any girl in the whole world who has as wonderful a doll as mine. She's pretty wild, but I love her anyway. No one but I knows that she can talk and laugh and eat just like a regular human being. When Mama and Papa are nearby, she stares straight into the air and doesn't look one bit alive. But when we are alone together, we have the best time.

She loves waffles. I have a doll waffle iron, and I bake waffles for her every day. Mama thinks that I'm just pretending that Mirabelle eats, but she really eats. One time she even bit my finger—just for fun, of course.

Papa has made her a little bed so she doesn't have to sleep in the sewing machine cover. Mama has sewn sheets and a quilt for her. And I have made her a fancy nightgown, aprons, and an everyday dress. Mirabelle loves to get new things. I play with her all day long except when I have to help Papa weed the garden.

Every time I hear a cart in the lane, I rush to the gate to see if it's the odd little old man coming by again. I would so much like to thank him for my beautiful, beautiful doll.

But he never comes.

Would you like to see my doll, my beautiful, elegant Mirabelle? Come and say hello to me and you'll get to meet her. Just follow the narrow lane that leads to our house. I promise I'll be standing at the gate with Mirabelle.